THE KNOPF POETRY SERIES

ALSO BY STEPHEN SANDY

Stresses in the Peaceable Kingdom
Roofs

Limited Editions

Caroms
Japanese Room
The Difficulty
End of the Picaro
The Hawthorne Effect
After the Hunt

Criticism

The Raveling of the Novel

RIDING TO GREYLOCK

RIDING
TO
GREYLOCK

Poems by Stephen Sandy

Alfred A. Knopf   New York   1983

THIS ... K
PUBLISHED ...)PF, INC.

Copyright © 1966, 1971, 1972, 19 ... 77, 1978, 1979, 1981, 1982, 1983

The poems in this collection wer ... d in the magazines listed below.
"Northway Tanka" and "Waiting ... originally appeared in *The Hudson
Review.* "Oyster Cove" originally appeared *in The New Yorker.* "Balance,"
"Declension," "End of the Picaro," "A Little Yard," "Sterling Mountain," "Survivor,
Walking" and "Winter Mountain" originally appeared in *Poetry.* Other selections
appeared in the following publications: *The Atlantic Monthly, Bad Henry Review, Blue
Buildings, Fire Exit, Iowa Review, Kayak, Michigan Quarterly Review, The Missouri
Review, New England Galaxy* (Old Sturbridge, Inc.), *New England Review, Paris Review,
Quarterly Review of Literature, Salmagundi,* and *Silo.*
"Cyanotype" originally appeared in *After the Hunt,* a chapbook published by
Moonsquilt Press.
Grateful acknowledgment is made to the following for permission to reprint from
previously published material:
Houghton Mifflin Company: "Shore" from *Roofs* by Stephen Sandy. Copyright ©
1971 by Stephen Sandy. Reprinted by permission of Houghton Mifflin Company.
The Nation Associates: "Some Flowers" by Stephen Sandy. Copyright 1968 Nation
Magazine, The Nation Associates, Inc.

My thanks to the Ossabaw Island Project, the Corporation of Yaddo, the Vermont
Council on the Arts, and Bennington College for giving me time to begin a number
of these poems.

Library of Congress Cataloging in Publication Data
Sandy, Stephen.   Riding to Greylock.
(Knopf poetry series; 11)
I. Title.
PS3569.A52R5   1983   811'.54   82-48741
ISBN 0-394-52819-0
ISBN 0-394-71314-1 (pbk.)

Manufactured in the United States of America

FIRST EDITION

for Virginia

CONTENTS

I V

I

END OF THE PICARO

The path strewn with leaves, lined with kempt bushes
Behind which someone languished for salvation

The path that trailed off in the confining
Attenuations of perspective (which alone
Seemed to beckon and comfort) the wanderer
Before a cut stone wall stalled in wonder

Where in the stones were hewn fragments of letters
QR, VT, and so forth: so that even
A picaro soon saw what he had come to

The something larger he'd been thrown up out of
As these remains of masonry still grander—
Edifice once of stunning proportions—decked
With mottos of obedience, loyalty, pomp:
But now the lesser from the greater ruin.
Some eighteen feet or more where tendrils grip
The scattered letters broken to unbreakable
Code. The trail stops here.
                    Or here. And here.
Or so: it merely fails in brakes where kudzu
Wild grape and raspberry lashes rope and knot.

In much the same way your knack of finding
                    in the picaro what you desire:
To have his scrapes
His trips & happy tangos with relenting ogres
Means what you desire because to begin with
You sent him forth. You never had to open a book

And always he smiled over his shoulder
The musket propped against a birch while he
Laced up his buskins, Gil smiled forever
At you following
            letting you know he knew:
A genie of daydreams, loyal, obedient, true.

His fealty was the important part
And no converging symmetrical plot imposed
            by an author who
In his closet wisdom
Made plot subserve your quest. But you, the you
Shackled within
                  who would pay out, be picaro
Never content to play some anecdotal bit
Part in the corporate folly history,
Venerable rosary. Here your youth
Stymied at the stricken plot of the world
Stands at the edifice eternity
Defaces and like an Asian god, with eyes
Averted, effaces himself and doubles back
And homeward, down tangled banks, to your first need.

FREEWAY

Wind swims the pines
         a screech owl sleeps the sun,
fat trout of noon,
tail-swing answering branch-sway.

Dark waves totter in forest light,
         trunks of shadow, cones.
Deep, the anemones bloom.

    The Cat plows, fangjawed, a Hyster Roller
    pleats the loam; stones clang
    on drums. Steel.
    Cement layers, barechested, approach
        twelve yards a day.

The breakers pound.

AT PEAKS ISLAND

There on the tangle of granite planes
And mica glintings, on the torn
Wrappings of sunlight and a cord of crystal
Tying an edge, someone had left
Beside a patch of lichen and a square of moss

A box of Binney & Smith Crayola crayons, *carnation*
Pink, sea green, periwinkle, burnt sienna
Half a *maize,* a stub of *sky*
Blue. They looked
Ready to use again
After a musing child had colored in a lichen
Or dotted the nightshade with purple dots;
The box of colors seemed to lie there ready
To turn a pebble red or blue, to heighten a petal: but not

To spray "Lucy Grillo Loves George Rockwood"
In dumb letters on the face of the concrete
Bunker down the shore, this dated rockery
For men to spot the Nazi U-boats from;

And least of all to be taken up
To draw the seascape, stubs too blunt
For noon, for a horizon, or
The join of plane and fracture.
(I took them, I tried to capture

Those minimal, burning edges
Of magnitude. The page became
A jam of trails blindly grappling
Unending volumes, as warped with accident
As a child's map of seeing.)

❖

Summer people here
Gather along the shore road at sunset
Or wade in Spar Cove
And know where not to hang their monickers: not
On the scoured knee of a rawboned sea cliff, not to color
The unknown, reserving their penchant to say
"Bernie Loves Minta" for the bunkers they know
Where uncles waited for years at the ready
With radios, Spam, the letters from home, the blankets
Lining each olive-drab nest

And watched the convoys from Portland gliding
To the contested seas, guarded by these
Concrete towers, dazed with amnesia now, long-haired
Stone faces under sumac and beach grass;
Or the warren of deep-tunneled loggias for guns
Below. There my desire
To wander knew no end. There
The shadows cling, damp with old toil,

Secrecy, absence. Anonymous, empty gun-bays
Receive a spray of naming now, "Civitarese
& Conkey," "Robin Rottin Crotch," and even
"Mein Fraülein ist auch shön."

I turned to you once, standing alone
On a parapet frowsy with daisies
While the last islanders sauntered toward their porches,
The outline of your peaceful shoulders, scintillant
In a fine dust of light from the banked sun rippling,
Burning westward over the rim of mainland.
(I took the *red violet,*
I drew it up my shin along the bone
And then with the piece of *nasturtium gold*
I wrote your name across my thigh.)

THE SCREEN

Light creeps between its legs. It keeps back
Dawn though, the sun that has not come. This dark
Suffices. He can see between the cracks.
He can hide there, behind it; it's nice and says

Offhandedly, *go away* to morning
And its scaffold of struts. Or shields two lovers
Taped shut by their dreams
From the madder light leaching

Toward this valley, the steel jaw of ridge
Holding its teeth to the sun. A sun wearing
A gray general's helmet with one star
Edging up, vast, above ramparts; beyond the sill.

He wakened, nevertheless, without a mask
To keep the light from his eyes.
Some light! "Are you here
At last?" he murmured. "I am sorry

You were not here before. Let me know
Let me touch your face, before I slip
Around the screen and go onto the hills, night
Shouldering its yoke, day with its Roman nose."

FAMILY ALBUM

The moonless night an apple tree in May
Snowing its distant faltering white
Across the darkness where we sleep upright

These sculptures are volcanic rock
Carved to look like corrugated card
The silly grin means they were once aflame

Your body hangs beneath your brain
A baggy marionette from strings
The owner's fingers move, it moves

The blind boy will not sing the song you want
You thought his eyes were only closed
In ecstasy. But the mouth his voice is using

Is holding forth for food, real food.
He cannot feel the shadow of your head
Fall on his shoulder when he sings his song.

Some wide-winged bird is hovering behind
Funneling the iced-milk propaganda
Down from the darkness where you sleep upright.

This sun and lilacs make us laugh right out
And then we pass without acknowledgement
Someone you love had written you a letter

And forgotten perhaps to sign it *love*
A total stranger gropes you and you scamper
You don't get even the name, only the eyes.

In Yucatan this spring is always there
The round stone faces timeworn strangers
Stare like ice-cream vendors through the vines

You see your brother and his parents
Dim stiff images that come through only
When held just right against the light

Iridescent in sun and figured velvet
Small merchants puffing for ambrotypes
The blind boy a blossom at their feet.

CYANOTYPE

A cat no one can see is sleeping in the blue
Corduroy of weeds. The boy we watch
Is feeding his pup affection, lounging where
The huge rock makes their place. From any angle

It's Sunday, a break for light. The cows become
Birch trees. A fragrance, June perhaps, settles
On a whole week faltering back to a lassitude
Of random stupors. A lime wash of the primeval

Haloes this homestead and its starch, this swatch
Shaved as a golf green, the velvet youth half clad
With shade. Aspens carefully dangle their
Little tongueless bells. At the right a man

In a derby holds his hands as if about
To punt a ball; a black skin satchel hangs
From his shoulder. Now the boy dissolves, and the rock
Swallows the dog: in its folds they know a recess.

In her house behind the granite outcrop a woman
Shrimps dripping hands across her muslined mangle.
She has no more now to do by rote unless
It is to rise and turn to boil more laundry

Then their dinner. There in the buckled pasture
Two shapes, besides the beech stumps, linger on.
The yawning dog and the boy in his Fauntleroy suit
Manage to stay. A breakthrough. The man and his mad

Pallor have vanished. Already beyond the rails
Of fear, we can relax now with the blue boy
Not panicked, careful not to startle the sun
Absently caressing its side of his body.

GROUPINGS

At Sagamore, above the rocks in shreds,
A Staffordshire party in holiday attire
Camps on the widow's mantel. Noon invades
Her living room, blades from the sea. Each knickknack

Glitters in tartan, frock coat, tucked velure.
Not one a lingering Eve; not remotely Adamic,
These tourists with lambs, forever out of place.
The lady turns to her picture window. Huge

Gulls lounging; an assembly of sandpipers taking
The air. They saunter till they rush; they tease
The quiet friaries of the surf. Touching the curtain
She takes the view in. Each outline calms her nerves,

Each part of the horizon. Down the boulder
Garden of the beach, the man in the Norfolk jacket
Goes walking again, poking his cane at the beryl
Mouths of quahogs gaping for spray. The ceramic

Shepherds and maids, she thinks, have no such waking,
No day to run in like the shore birds, back
And forth. Her figurines enclose their little
Vaults of air that held them steady in the fire

Of a kiln which left them final, gleaming, brittle.
The fire in the grate is humming, warm and certain;
Her dog on the hearth is dry now; sleeps, secure
From dispositions of odd weathers, the racket

Of breakers where clam and periwinkle molder,
Shored on the chamois kelp, suede weed, or lace
Of sand. Neither menagerie persuades
Her still desiring eyes, when one deluge

Looms like another. Both these groupings please
For having pushed their health beyond reserves;
Those little folk, shelved from their quilted beds,
Going more gray, calmly approachable.

EAGLE BRIDGE FARM

Her master done with riding now
a white mare lightly trots
over the sugar-snow. She moves to us
the film clip of her escape
being played backward;
lithe, her zigzag of approach!
And we, unwired freedom or some
limitless West on the horizon in her eye?

But we have only visited this place
and may not share it with her, acres
that we explore, unfolding,
that their owner would have us own.
Where stubble leaches from the March
slush, a bank plummets to dark water
through loggias of hemlock and birches solving
the sudden space.

The milkhouse gleams
a collection of stainless instruments
huddled for auction. A hayrake
cages saplings. Year by year
the gorge deepens, hemlock roots
gnarl in air.

A white mare against fresh snow
has shed her white, lessens
from mounts tall and ivory in sunlight
to a yellow horse
dung on her fetlocks.
The farm is going. Everything
keeps being only our knowledge of it.

Last the river,
olive with ice floes.

LOOKING ON

The first leaves flickered, he noticed shade blurred
Along the slope; the light on the hill was soft as flannel
With buds. He knelt there
To pull pigweed and stray bush-clover from the bed

Where Doily spiders overnight had raised
Splendid tents along the plants
And moss, now gauze-wrapped malachite.
And the fennel they were given last year

That didn't take and they had given up for dead
Was back, minutest nebulae of white
Stars in the shallows of green, by chance
Filling a patch now one yard square, a panel

Of shadows. He hadn't seen her come, nor heard.
And she was by him now, her shadow there almost
Covering him, melding where others grazed
His downturned head. He felt this when the air,

Oiled with a licorice odor, held—then stirred
Slight as the flash of a finch's wing yet clear
As the salt breeze once, in Maine, on a rock coast
In the crash of waves, and a gull's cry overhead.

SHADOW

My father comes to the window
where I am standing, looking
at the trees. His Oxfords shined
with wax and his own spit are dark
and quick as a pair of eyes.
My father looks at the trees

not me and says, after silence,
teach me things, what you've done
with these years. He stands there
his eyes fastened on the boughs
billowing in the wind beyond.
There the hoofs of horses churn

pawing the surf of morning
the manes of the horses rising
in the neighing wind of speed;
they are the stones of mountains smoothed
by the saw-toothed ice
cast into granite furbelows;

they are huge geodes of desire
loitering above their roots
tied to the truth of their earth;
in the starry night the shapes
of the trees are black mouths
rending the sky with their need;

and now I remember the salads
of memory tossed by love

and heavenward boughs windshaken
causing the circles of shade beneath
to blur, to shift,
undulant shades of despair

held in while the sun browns the fields
rolling like fresh-baked loaves out
to the arms of the sky.
My father stands at the window,
he does a little soft-shoe step
for a moment, unsmiling, agile

as he peers out at the whole view
silent, through the grid of sash.
His shadow falls across me,
gently it brushes my arm
with a surmise of the cold
waste my eyes have entertained.

ARCH

These hands that
in the sunlight
extemporize
shielding themselves
from a crowded street
a minor frieze
of the untouching body

These eyes
that are the body
going out from itself
like water reaching
for a level

This loam earth
where cold roots
knit fallen leaves
or cradle
unwitting seed

This is your season
your careless nature.

FLIGHT OF STEPS

Though [La Pietra] had been bruised and abandoned, the
garden had assumed a patina as of antique bronze, as if it
had been standing on the hillside since the seventeenth cen-
tury. . . . This was the background of my boyhood and we
had grown up together. . . . weeds burst through the cracks
and forced their way through the pebble-patterned stairways;
the stone vases were empty, the gates were coated with
rust. . . . I could not see it again with the innocent eyes of
my youth but thoughts and emotions long dormant came
drifting back.

                         —Sir Harold Acton

1

Farewell, then, to this
      Residue of place, their styled
Concessions dapper
      With tattersall and webbing
Lounges; the kiosk
      Of junk! The folks smile on; they
Quaff tall drinks on their
      Decks imbrued with creosote
Bossed with loud statues
      And raw-glass insulators.

For aftermath, the catatonic apartment.
      In the roominghouse yard a scrap of snow in mud.
A bare arm hanging out of a window, or one
      Dirty big toe, cold at the mouth of a broken
Shoe. Budweiser cans, three grapefruit skulls under the
      Window of the girl painter.

2

On the edge, having
    About had it, he cried, "I
Might have given out
    Life, or the slice I cherished
To *Progress*." And now
    Even as he is about
To be left alone
    He wants this: to lose his place.

You laughed, and the match
    For your smoke went out once more.
Laughing was over-
    Flow. It parleyed with the flame
Saying, "I'll make the flame here."

3

    Look here: his black tracks
Grow larger, swell as snow melts
    —Frankenstein trekking
North. Yard-long boot shapes pool, merge
    With the salty Interstate.

    Lithe hours havoc
And absorb each drift; footprints
    Vanish into each
Other. Remember the rings,

Grass around tree trunks
Come spring, pressing out as if
    To settle summer's
Limit of shade? Direction
    Erases itself.
Perspectives extend. A time
    Destructs, flame blown to zero.

4

He never thought this raging furnace of the head
    Would get him beyond
And yet he did. He mumbled, or considered how
    All wordings of it scrambled.

When you wrote under
    Maples at a worn picnic
Table you found one
    Knothole, knot long gone, plugged now
    By paper, marked with faint words.

5

The clouds like Indians
    On snowshoes with bowstrings taut
Absorb the traces,

Pick off great destinies. He
Might make himself scarce
    Now, smoothe over his brushstrokes,
Try for an exact
    Anonymous mid-distance.

After Sunday's frost
    Under the white pines, a fresh
Carpet of needles
    Dry, smooth, slippery. He slides,
        Leather soles skate over them.

6

A kind of peace spilled
As if everything that he
Counted on had split
    Underground, the good pictures
The fair legs, the gifts
    (Not overwhelming perhaps
But choice) survivals
    From a terrace more ample
With lemons and box
    Hedges among these mellow
    Cinders of his lot, gifts—not
Memories quite—that

Had been a matter of life
Bequeathing him hope
 Through the salvos of wise smiles
 And the shined quarters of prose.

7

 Through fur-twigged sumac
One jay rules. Jay, jay, brainy
 Bird, you hammer out
Your protocols unheard. One
 Jag of blue against
Greens; loud at strewn umbers, at
 Rifle green, greens deeper still!

ANNIVERSARY SONNET

The hawk above boxes the blue compass of his flyway,
below in their dusty temples the mice bow down
before the eye in the pheasant's tail
and the gold earrings of the corn.

A man was calling his dog in the distance, calling.
The last drops on mossed rock tell the hour
down the viridian micro-scape, a carillon
where a patch of mist hovers behind the willows
an edgeless whiteness
like a woman discovered in her bath half hoping half

shrinking to appear. Your fears turned, coiling
upward like ash afloat in the fire of generation
when you curled up, so
small, and I gave you sleep.

FINISHED COUNTRY

The bat stretches a puce wing
The forest lays down its arms
Snow has mounted the hemlock bough
And a bouffant catafalque on April wires.
Your friends are facing the other way
The mountain's waist is zoned in mist

The orphan seizes the day
The sevens keep coming.
The snake's eyes peer
From under mossy eyebrows
Where roots rock back on their heels
Where chevrons of the blackbird signal.

Gears meshed: they took
Arthur and made him President
His peeling birthplace lingered upstate
The stream smoked from white tie and tails.
Lavender tongues of early bearded iris
Ride the green spears, vulva, dolphins,

The empty crater of a grapefruit half
Shines on the trash heap, a reeking sun.
And Lust goes about his weekly shopping
In splintered glasses: frolicking
Mongrels at fresh scents pause with longing eyes
The ill-begotten tangle in wettest light.

IN THE DAKOTAS

The head of a fence post glances
splintering in the sun.
A season; wooly bears creep West,
they vanish with his wheels.

A winded rose lies torn from the wall,
mist trails from the pine lot
where he, departing, calls
Mother, calling her one name,

a whole grammar of longing
where cowled autumns hover.
The wet macadams, iridescent,
give back smears of light

blueprints of
spring's butterflies.

THIS CHILL AIR

Each leafless apple tree
in starlight, on snow crust
made the same gesture

Each braid of barked branches
from knots onward reaching
held to the still turmoil of aging

Each branch turned in rising
as flames riding, tongue-leaps
turned in the wind to one song

All the branches against night
straining to hold
to the null cold and final star:

A man walks that orchard dead
like a roach madly circling
the laths of a house twisting to ashes

Smoke as the black joints creak upward.

❖

In this chill air
and no hurry
I see unusual distances

Heavy, heavy
knowing their time
the boughs of the apple bend downward

Today I am
keeper of a peace inside and out

The tree, laden
shines with intent of being itself.

RIVERBOAT

Dejection is labor-intensive, you see not feel.
It is easier to turn tail by the stove, the one
Purring blackness, inside with the folks smiling.
But now that the curtain has been drawn back you see

In the storm pane the picture above your head, which you
Had not looked at for months, for years: at twilight
On a river in mountains the riverboat glows with warm
Cabin lanterns, men pole it onward to the West

Where gray cloud foams over the orange sun
And little tinks of laughter waft from the gray craft
In its slow progress. Ah, what is in your eyes,
Blankard, clinging as a frightened child's?

World to a close at last? The flares of laughter
Have no bed, as I-beams do, driven to rock before
The pouring begins. Your laugh, and my laugh too,
Like opened fans in separate cases on the wall.

TOM AND HENRY, CAMPING OUT

Well, Ford, people like us, we
Don't have to worry. We have the river
Coming up just here. Dancing came

Naturally, easy as misprint in a bunch
Of kids setting their own type. We had
Palazzo font, and the right note

Of resignation. To find purple gauze
Or gold faience on morning coffee means
The whole day will go by like a nap.

We had the cherry flowering above us
Where we lounged like arrived mallards
The voluble petals billowing

Around us whispering, "How far is down?"
We had a candle ready and watched the lightning
Shred up from the landing field in the valley

When the transformer went. You laughed,
"Never explain." We knew if we could step out
Of our bodies they would fill up with those garnets.

II

NATIVITY

Cnly husbands wearing gowns
permitted beyond this point

—Maternity ward sign

A picture-windowed fifth-floor room:
above the rubble of delivery tables
the rubber sheets and terry towels
tray and stirrup, clamp and bolt,
a kind contraption shows the portal of your womb.
Among the arc lights everywhere
a convex mirror hung
above us like a shield
mediates, enlarging this far-flung
spectacle. May we not miss
the moment, paradise
of generation verified; *now* made minutely visible!

From slippery boards where we had danced
cobwebbed performers growing old
two seniors of Shalott feeling the cold
together we observed right breathing through the fast.
Suddenly lost
finding your own, as in a dream, you cry at last.
Dumbfounded spirits then, entranced
and hand in hand, a doubled Perseus,
behold this stun-
ning end of one.
The mirror returns
its image of

one love
becoming two; the utterly sumptuous
revolt.

You watch Medusa slowly wakening from sleep to flood
this gate of bone shifting to yawn in larger
gapes of you; and soon
the crown, like a shadow moon
through mist, appears
ghostly lanugo and bone, the chromium charger
with clamps like fangs, drenched hair
and plume of blood
and how you lost
—cried *No!*, your fare-thee-well to years
when the last great Hokusai wave, towering, tossed
you back, combed through us there
with rifling fold
furling along that shore
of incandescent light.
With distance doubled by the brilliant shield
we watch it yield
no stone, no harm, but suffered bliss.
Hard looking has afforded this.

The dazzled retina, then the Persian blue
sky I saw that shone above your head.
Stars and planets gleamed, spun
in one
boreal candelabrum,

shone out far from the saddle and the sheet
lighting a way, this exile from
ourselves, this passing through.

When all was done
twin cries declared what had begun:
your own, and this anomalous squinting incubus
a magnum of champagne uncorked
such great nothings-to-do-with-us!
Forgotten now in that hospitable tumult
we were begotten too. Henceforward forked:
pinned on our astonished tines,
that business, this result:
one sociable camp meeting
or stairway of a summer night—
and now, surprised by her small muscular hello's,
we greet our own charisma, anodyne;
three rare birds flushed to flight
under one sign.

AFTER

Do not Enter; Babies
are with their Mothers

—Hospital sign

The latticed creel of morning

    charts through wicker bars

Its warming light across
    this born other
        in modest shock

    still chastened by her loss
        in whom deep sleep alone
        is seeing stars!

❖

My child is only sleep

    and I am high
        on fatherhood
        looking down

Sleepless and shaggy as a sheep
Graceless, nearly useless: but standing by

my post, a greater
from a lesser
good the witness.

Foot on rim
Gets footing for the other
On Death's equivocal, slippery crater

far from the plain below
where mother is the mother
is the mother

resting, burning low.

POSTPARTUM BLUE

"A lichened marble lady at the Villa Casino,
Carved by prisoner Turks two hundred years ago,
I saw her." The voyage of all rock to dust or water.
The tunnel collapsing back, uncertain ruins.

Off in the other room, a market place;
Cries of bartering, far. Cries among drifting
Timber dreams, drifting ashore; the fresh
Indenture, the worn lip on an alien threshold.

Beached from the wrench of him now parted from her
She dreams of vegetables ripe in mounds; a war
At sea, howls of the Venetian sailors drowning,
The bloody slap as, one by one, packing

Their lungs with air, those bodies hit the water.
The lichened marble lady at the Villa Casino,
The voyage of all rock and dust to water,
Tunnels collapsing, a burial of ruins.

MITHUNA

They were
cedar waxwings side
by side, helmeted;
two sparrows (English)
in mufti
        elm by
elm, mute snow coasting;
cardinals clearing
for winter; or one
pair crows in clean kit:

never on a branch
together attend
each other.
        The fanned
feathers of the tail
hold down aft the bark

where twig hands sternly
prehensile argue
the cowled weathers for
judgments of balance.

So the wall-eyed stares
offer in answer
steady pulls

and tail
feathers, opposed con-
cerns, peg in space those
tents of their bodies.

Even with such trained
severe responses
always when one bird
watches its mate or
(merely) another

the second cannot
return the regard
received, unable
to acknowledge such
communion of air:

but watches, watched, sway-
ing with the mast of
the tree, focuses
(as if so much was
worth his life) with a
sensible bead on

a thorn or mote in
the thicket of air,
a spore of deer moss
or the green aphid
of a rose.

WHEN APRIL

Like blown Venetian glass
beads of rain hang there
cling, brittle, with yellow

buds, prehensile pickets
of April or bird song
on the forsythia branch.

Not moving quite they probe
hour by hour the cold
drenched light where, below

already the purple
or golden para-
chutes of crocus droop.

The pinstripe lavenders
and saffron soaked through,
limp. And you rest firm

as an August peach, soft
fell in our lamplight,
grip my finger like

a branch until your finger-
tips, smaller than
the rain clinging

to the mahogany lilac
twig, turn white.
Helpless remembering;

the branch; the root. You hold
on, or startle—
snapping your limbs at our cold

touch. You are one
week old today one week of this
dream enduring

and you turn
your false smile onward
to the brown

obedient nipple
waiting to serve
your quick, conjuring reflex.

MAKING IT UP

Her eyes one day are open. No more blinks,
Occulting takes of us. The stare hovers
Between lamp and wall. The survey stops
At the face that rides, grinning, into her ken.

With a remorseless reticence she looks
At his shaggy, doting smile—or proud Mt. Rushmore
Profile he has turned, as if to show her
His good side. She apes defiance, the serene

Cringe of one captured, fist clenched, looking up
At his face. In a while he turns away. He sees
A *kouroi,* colossal, fallen, the pitted marble
Head knocked off by vandals, genitals

Profaned. The old man takes the form of his
Experience on. She finds him there unmasked
In this stare that holds him, stare by which he knows
He too must make up now a life, unasked.

A LITTLE YARD

Sunlight hugs the walls.
The house is ticking. Winter's
Cardiac arrest.

Spring now; you can read
In the garden. Then you use
One sock for bookmark.

From the stump of the
Old willow, shoots arch, saffron
Stem and leaf. Clare, just
Two, sits there in shade, hands in
Her lap. "What Clare do!" she cries.

The bumble bee scouts
Me; moves on. I rest now, no
Flower after all.

You disappear then
To leave just us together.
The violets you
Were picking lie on the walk
Strewn from here to the back door.

Clare mounts the picnic
Table, sprawls on the warm height;
Copying the cat.

UNDER THE EAVES

The child knows the tap on slates of rain
As mother typing. His desires keep.
The broth of this moment, if you please.
He sucks on his bottle, world he's made.

Or, he cranes up to the typewriter keys,
Presses so many as will, when squashed
In a stack, stand together. They stood—
And the rain turned South. The stone it washed

The dust from is green, an oval jade.
And the child goes napping, dreaming rain
Holding the stone in his serious sleep
An hour, a stone he has named for good.

CONDENSATION

A wisp of straw hangs from
    The apple branch. On his window
Condensation blurs his
    View, couples walking by the
    River. Apples, spilled by the wall.

This autumn plenty. There,
    White noise from the heart. And no one
To hear the old voices,
    The singing. The cricket crutches
    Moonward from the cooling hearth. This

Small clamor in his blood
    Is somehow some small knowledge of
His child: which will become
    A protean encroachment on
    The petty dark of solitude.

Possession is nine-tenths
    Of the disenchantment. The hills
Go platinum with frost.
    He could remember keeping score,
    All those affections in a row

Then letting them go. And
    Letting go, he let time alone.
Only the windy young
    Have nothing in common, although
    They share findings. They find common

Cause against calendars
    And fear another hand on the
Misted pane where, smiling,
    A girl peers in on them, a gold
    Leaf in her damp, night-tangled hair.

YOUNG MAN WITH INFANT

Surprised, you think: respond to his cry; you feel
That wailing cries to you. The ark of nightfall
Sweeps past, the window lights go black. An iron
Crunch of snow; wood ash on heels from the dark

Pocking the rug with smudges. It does not matter
That he is not thinking of you, but crying
Some stone of air away. She nurses him
Then lights the candles. Saffron trees from flames

Rise by the stove from shadows. The picture
Of love, may be; or the scrawl of affection surviving.
His sister champs for Bear to fight with Monkey.
Laughter and roughhouse. "Bear fights till Bear wins."

Down the lake, ice cracks; hurtles to the wincing dark.
Flies cling to the ceiling, stalled. A tureen of warmth
Through quartered, steaming panes you might find here
Below the winds that creak through zero's midnight.

STORM-FELLED TREE
AT EAGLE BRIDGE

for John Ford Noonan

Faces of wood chips yet
Pliant with being limb;
Arcade of branches zeroed,

Smashed chalices of green.
The grounded light! Bright splints
And chain-sawed meal cascade

Burying moss where a black
Brigade of ants scurries,
Orders changed. The air,

Emptied. A sea at noon,
Emerald escalade
On the inked bank of white!

The oak lies wreckage of
Itself, each slab a slow
Grenade; then ember; smoke;

That heats, like an old love
Played through once more,
The pale house it shaded.

GLORIES OF THE WORLD

It is time to learn a new word, children; wait.
It is the syllable of tears, yet nothing special.
Your faces each are perfect as a Sèvres plate,
All the right edges, not a blemish, yet

You two must understand, like a treadle pair
Of roots that press where they must press—onward,
And blind. (The light would numb them.) The car is ready
Yet the trouble with going some place, finally,

Is being there. The mountains rise beyond the hills,
This landscape where you have always never been.
A streak of late light clips one cardboard corner.
Your eyelids fold like the field turned down for winter.

"I know how much you love me, and you don't."
"You can't have this without catastrophe."
Instead, you do. Instead. "I might be sad
Thinking my love is not those miles away."

SURVIVOR, WALKING

to Malcolm Cowley

He knew the stories he could tell
    Like his own garden—well.
And then he knew the woods, could tame
    Each wildness with a name.
    Fondly he rapped the knees
    Of ancient, familiar trees

With his green beechwood hiking staff.
    Their silence swelled his laugh
As he saluted those careers
    He'd followed forty years.
    Half rot, half youthful still,
    Growth was their only skill.

"Across this trunk note how the sun
    Shows burnished cinnamon."
(His loud, half-deaf discourse.) "The bark
    No longer looks just dark,
    It lives a hundred years
    Or so, till this appears."

Growling in anger once, he stopped
    Before some spruces lopped
(Years back) at the neck for Christmas trees.
    He cried, "Now look at these
    Some bastard has got at!
    Who'd do a thing like that?"

One birch, in a woodlot maples won,
    Leaned there, a veteran

Stripped naked, where its sun had failed.
    Even this one he hailed
    Like an impoverished friend
    Remembered to the end.

At home, on trees pulped down, he wrote
    Critique and anecdote.
Working out front, working backstage
    He chronicled his age
    And by this balanced act
    Delivered up the fact.

On walks he still hails trees recalled
    By name, or stops, enthralled
By one no logger has cut down
    And lightning missed, whose crown
    Rails yet against the sky,
    Still at it, green and spry.

He will not hear us, not by half.
    Silences make him laugh.
Beyond our powers to persuade
    He drops his hearing aid
    And marches to the woods
    To join his earthly goods.

PREFECT

Windrose
of upland clearing

lichened outcrop
each crevice

bubbling moss
milk quartz-

notched granite
nudging sheep-

cropped grass
coppery

tip of earthcrust
dry rose

petals sailing
volumes of lean

Pleistocene air
comb turf, the blue

juniper tongues
all one way

I the other
look back,

perfect
stranger.

III

NORTHWAY TANKA

White leaves, magenta
leaves, curled in grass. A brown mesh
of needles, freshly
spread. One opened husk, the nut
tucked safe in a secret place.

❖

Sun struts from cloud then:
now mica stars stream past, make
macadam twinkle
racing under, around me;
mighty pines of night, each side.

❖

Over the cleared fields
striding and mountain shadows
stream, draining earth's warmth.
Outside, a dog whines.
A clear sky, cleared for winter.

❖

Black spaces under pines.
Ahead, a vast cold front, cloud
range level, half to
zenith: a wall of winter
at the far end of the world.

❖

Blind as pain these men
stand, stretching by their parked cars.
Hoods shine apart where

beyond mountains swim into
the great mandala of light.

❖

Dolorous granite
rock like a crouching lion,
tumbled by glaciers!
Rock like a crouching lion
rock like a crouching lion!

❖

A shred of cloud trails
the mountain face; catches
on a pine: below
a striped lump that is, that was
raccoon; and one Piels beer can.

❖

Lifted from its bed
by a passing wind the leaf
raised the brown profile
of a chipmunk. Then it sank
back; but stood again; again.

❖

To stand in a field
silenced and drained for winter

where one clover blooms
and hear, muffled by distance,
the geese calling for summer!

Ribboning silence
they keep forming, keep a long
communal mewing.
I stood there when I heard this
wan assumption of their cries.

❖

The two-rut dirt road
trailed from the four-lane highway
dissolving shortly
in dense toils, second-growth scrub.
My country, O my country!

❖

When it was summer
the long rain fell silently
soaking grass and earth:
now on beds of brittle leaves
cold rains tattoo ceaselessly.

❖

Still in place the leaves
of a poplar, lime and gray,

simmer together
on the wind. A squall flaps them,
the words blow up off my page.

❖

I walk these dry paths
under bare branch and bare sky.
Through the leaves' ruin,
churning loudly, my feet go.
With snow, this too will be stilled.

❖

When I drove southward
through trees ranked on a ridge crest
the sun, setting, West,
paced me: a rapid fire
stuttered between trunks stock still.

DECLENSION

In the chorus of memories a blessing in disguise.
The birds and the trees are satisfied. If these
Appear to grow smaller with distance how
Tell of the particulate the towering
Matter of the pine, its needles, or its osprey
Waiting magnanimous upon the sun
You saw from the curl of the bend back-rising there?

The tree, its mossed feet, the mane green:
Manor for whom, for what? The bird, or song
You had to ignore, heading on. A death?
Not knowing, you ignored the tree, the osprey.
What is not yours is that beyond the time
You do; or might be; or, "Once upon a time. . . ."

Spare, untouchable, the river bank. And there
White water, phrasing, races past you, back.
Particular roadside pines, converging walls
Backing the head—to vanishing point. A sense
Of acrid pine musk that might have been there lingers,
Remembered. The graceful ornaments linger on
And overwhelm.
                    How then will you get on
To what you know, as you must? The eggshell
On the garden path; the tanager's intent
In tapering branches? All this is what is not
For you, and the words rise outward toward your smile.

RIDING TO GREYLOCK

Two schoolboys behind still talk
about their winter vacation
while I ransack my bags.
Here is my Edwardian
boy's nature book, "The Romance
of Animal Crafts," but the Mohawk

Trail has seen better days,
our Bonanza bus zigzags
an icy curve; no one
could read now. And I admit
it: I have lost my keys.
They're gone. So here I sit

desiring them, wondering
in which snowdrift they are.
Across the hills Mt. Greylock
hulks like a beached whale,
flooded by air. The bare
branches mullion the fields.

Coupin writes how curious
the nests of field mice were,
houses woven at home,
ingenious; neat. Are mice
unreconciled as us
to losing things in the snow?

There's no romance in ant
hotels you can be sure,

nor in these great showplaces
of the pleasing coral polyps.
But if their buildings can't
leave me a vision of

myself, forget them. The dams
of the sedulous, crafty beaver
delight me. Soon I note
a "beaver vernacular";
then in her tale for children
some spinster gives them trappings

—hearth rugs and pillow shams,
the sort of thing we heard
and half believed in childhood.
Then, we compared our lot
with the beaver or the witch,
thought hard which one we'd choose

to be (and which was which!).
It's dangerous to think
of animals as stuffed
toys, stunted people; just as
children, carefully coiffed
and propped in old photos

—baby fogeys—are hideous,
vain midgets like Tom Thumb.
All this is fallacy
of course; pathetic and

old hat. How did I come
to this? Because I feel

defenseless today? A fish
out of water, a snail
without a shell? A boy
without his key!
                    They've turned
the heat off now; it's cold.
That wakes you up! I wish

I had not watched the old
lady in black on the ice
outside the bus collapse
in stroke or heart attack!
When I stopped there, too near,
I saw each ebbing synapse

snap; her face pass fear,
stiffen and loosen at once,
blue with the deep eye-shadow
of death. That lying there
like a rag doll grown huge,
adulterated, slack

at the seams (as where the rouge
spots on her cheeks seemed cotton
patches coming loose),

that had to happen. But
to think of someone dying
becoming some recluse

of his old self, and gladly!
What if she had been able
and willing? A priest had called
for her name (he must perform
last rites) and no one helped.
The crowd was behaving badly.

Maybe the lady chose
it this way, ready to shed
her frilly skin; to lie back,
savaged. The willingness
of an animal to be dead
when it must; a flower's; the dog's

eye in a fading rose!
        These fields half overgrown
lie caulked with snow now, choke
on their abandoned bones
of stalk and stubble. The bus
rocks me; or when I doze

knocks me awake. In Greylock's
shadow now, we're nearly there,

where I will hunt for my keys.
The boys are silent. Then, "O!
there was a fox, a red fox
on the soccer field! On the snow!"

WAITING FOR THE WARDEN

A doe like a brown empress
sitting at twilight there
in the snow watches the hounds gathering
        like retainers
slowly tracking the rise
bearing the gifts of blood
in their eyes.

Against sun falling past locust saplings
how serenely the doe looks out
        down the snowfield
chalked with dusk's blue!
Her shoulder is broken

        no pain: or
there is none I can see.

A bronze stillness letting death in
the unknown the fearful
the black shapes of hunters and dogs
        become the known
holding no fear longer
slowly approaching the cloud
one imagines before her eyes there
as breaths in the cold air.

I cannot tell how she accepted death
how beautiful
the long headlights of the warden's car
great tunnels through the dark and stillness.

STERLING MOUNTAIN

for Harry Mathews

Which would I choose? This week a mouse-gray stain
That bleach won't cancel is curling up the side
Of my flea-market mug, crazed Alton ware.
By Friday it should reach the lip. The girl
At lunch with chopsticks, mouthing cottage cheese,
Well knew no meat sufficed. The fact was, one
Did not need *food*. "This saint, a woman in
India, is completely free of vice:
No grain, no meat, no greens, no cup or curd
For sixty years: and gets her vitals from the sun."

I *know*. But chopsticks? "I'd rather have the taste
Of wood than metal on my tongue." And where
Had she wailed once for a brown nipple, I ask—
And think of Madeline; devout not meek; her slurred
Speech; to whom an angel did appear, at home,
In Morrisville, Vermont; in white, two feet
Above the floor, commanding her, *now love
And stop the slaughtering of animals.*
She would not let her father raise beef cows.
Death pained her. His vice; the massacre; this waste.

Like patches of sky against the green, the holy
Jerseys sway and munch, or chew and bask

Showing their bones like tent poles under tents
Of living leather, buff or chocolate; rich.
That farmer of Stowe who gently whacked his herd
Over Route 100, lunging slowly;
He saw rain coming, rain in bucketfuls
And did not pause to make us understand
In our cars, in the muggy wet. Then passage; breeze:
A day to be alive! I saw her hand

Pull at the air between us, imploring. Madeline,
One day you'll forget the angel, turning slow
As the herd to the soggy field, fenced off, to stitch
The burdock with teeth ground down to ivory knurls
Bedded in jawbone. Clouds hang, slack sails, above
Sterling Mountain. Gray shadows drape its walls.
Friday. Another stifling day. I hold still,
Facing my little window, its little slice
Of air. I bite my beef and want to know,
How will it go with these committed girls?

OYSTER COVE

The macadam is flaking and the lilac
Too big to bloom
Fingers a cobweb of smoky light from the terrace,
Grazes the sun-chalked cedarshakes. And no surprise.

Gone the lady, to Athens or Anjou. Her sunroom
Oozes silence. The paisley over the back
Of a wicker rocker. The pedals of her grand hover
Above the calm sea of the tiled floor

Like gilt clouds, each brazen ball
Without a claw. In Roseville jardinieres
Iron geraniums stiffen and chip;
A noose of rose and the scum of ferrous

Oxide throttle the sundial's Horatian tip
For those noddy panamas and white-ducks of class.
In the pergola woodflies on the pedestal
Walk all over it. What are years?

Or at the stoned gazing globe's crashed glass
Peek in on themselves, magnified; what's more,
Behold no Chloe nor her golfing lover
In the mullioned saucers of their eyes.

NEAR PAMET MARSH

Nothing was there
but branches, throwing
him off the track.
The last light was going,
the sun had gone;
only the gray char
of lichened bark
and the darker swaths

of hemlock bough.
He thought, "how banal is
that exquisite
white cedar now!"
The spiked mast towered
listing beyond repair
above him, no hint
of how to get back

or where the path went. It
divided, then angled
off both ways. Which
way? He had the dark
on his hands, a faint tar
to catch the ivy laced
over the swamp tract
like a chrysalis.

One beam to home on:
the chalcedony glint
from the muskrat's eye
in a net of wet

twigs, when the strip
of cloudbank scoured
all light from the tangled
ancient cowpaths.

There was dissension
with the night. At length
he stopped. An hour
and more he heard
the noise of space
that roared and reared
where the stars had spread
their barbed net. All

at once, the stitch
of a lamp through lampblacked
branches, the gilt-
edged beam a shred
of someone's hearth
that reached in friendship
(so it appeared)
across the quilt

of ground-pine down
to one who had faced
desolate palaces;
and found on the damp earth
a kind of bower
framing a tension
between his strength
and the waste that was.

SHORE

The stormbird
out, overhead,
circles in darkness. His ring
is inferred.

Up somewhere
out ahead
or behind this spit, lies his aim,
his need.

And gulls strain
on the sea-groin,
adze trawling their cries between stars
and white foam.

Their lone song
does, does belong
on this delta of the dark world.
All, they ring

out, they roam
pluming the stream
of wind, dervish of storm, shriven
of sensed doom.

I would know
how well they do
in the wheels they ride and the posts they keep,
here below.

WINTER MOUNTAIN

The successful man becomes a king, the failed
Denounced, a bandit; depicted in the hills.
That everything flatters the taste of the present.

Reject today because of increased policies,
Upstairs with the silent and intimate past,
It is not certain whether he had been a member
And remained, painting, until his head was snow-white.
Into old age the pastime kept him from court
The shadow of a mountain in a dream.

Windows that opened to the night were empty.

Pity the shrunken form of his splendid body.

The pheasant in a cage could not rise to light,
The valleys undergo always changes. His needs
Snowy gulls over the waves that love each other,
He grazes the light of the setting sun
On a rock ledge darkness sweeps beneath.
A cold front at the western border plunders.
Hours for *study* to register the feelings,
No book worth making that takes one year.

In light washes the days and months glide
To no end. Years waste. The way a man kills time,
His virtue. Rocky angles of a horse once splendid.
Snow mixed with rain in the interior sections.

AIR FOR AIR

In such a glut of light frozen above
The sea he could not sort or separate
Sunlight from snow. So in the spare finesse
Of body barking ever up its tree
Of hungers it went ill to separate
The one desire from Desire. Yet those

Serene, those incremental devastations
(So incidentally serene) spoke well
Spoke jealousy of air for air, the shrike
Of energy against Atlantic shore,
Of spirals shifting in one zenith. And there
The frozen heather, wreaths of beach grass blew.

This ring of orderings had to serve there, tallied
But got diffracted in his jealous eyes.
Nothing was then as it would be between
That land that wave that air, nothing he saw
Would he be like to see again it said
It said it said. Back from the wind, from sand

And back, he found the sky undoing snow,
Salt glaze of frost slowly relenting, gleaming
On pitch pine and scrub oak, beryl and umber.
A nuthatch darted, then zigzagged down a bole
Through shade, half shade, full noon and out of sight.
The one who watched that little star trek might

Believe (in his best interest) he would come
On such clear movement once again as once
Before; and in his treble sighting make

All of it understood; the twisted reds
That wind bowed cedars to, a light on the bark,
The silent nuthatch or the howling shrike,

Keeping these sensible in understanding
How these were here, how long they would keep there.
Wouldn't he offer a possessive eye
Wouldn't he pay another visit hearing
"Nothing is now as it shall be"? *Shall be,*
A voice continuing repeats, *shall be.*

BALANCE

Through the yellow leaves you go,
Alert to the three acres
Around you, and remember
All that you knew about
Hunting with bow and arrow.
You scan the woods for miles

For hours peaceful as Quakers.
Birches, like falling snow
In sunlight, blur. You hear
A squirrel or a finch.
Take aim. At last the bowstring
Cracks, loud. A deer flings

His half-acknowledging
Stare back at you. The last
Thing you learned: sit down,
One hour. How many spikes
Were there? He's ambled off!
A careful arrow strikes

Flank or hindquarter so
Lightly (though it will take
Hold, work deep) at first
The deer fails to notice
And flicks as if to shake
A fly off, or at worst

Shies back some yards; and goes
On grazing. Your presence must
Be known, if you begin

To track at once. Your quarry—
If you so much as flinch—
Takes flight; adrenalin

Will keep him up for miles.
If you have taken trust
From the October light
He'll find the time and wiles
To lose you, as he loses
Blood. But don't alarm him

And blood will slowly clot,
Slowly he will weaken
And quietly lie down
And, as the blood cools, find
He's rooted to the spot
Where he caught sight of you.

He will die there near you
Where with silent presence
You sat through it all
And did not move an inch,
Holding the animal
And your deed in level balance.

IV

THE AUSTIN TOWER

Charles Whitman, Texas, 1966

If I talked with you tomorrow.
But
    I have cut off my ear
My treasured lobe

No one will know

I cannot hear you anymore
In this
Music about music about music.

I have
Turned in all
My cards. There is

Too much organ music
In my ear.

            ❖

I came out of the rain, the train had stopped
The glass buildings spurted corn silk from rooftops
It was afternoon, I decided: *not in uniform.*
The city came up fast the din
Fell around like snow. The blizzard of

My sunlight. I spent a third of my life
Wearing my radio, wearing

My weaponry, gaining and
Losing.
There are stretch marks on my heart.

What empty vessels
Achievement patches from eagles
The barbecues of fighting or fitting
In, frail silks, nauseous, jockeying for wins
The red wins, long weeks learning to swim
With grace to shiver at their dock.

❖

This life is bluegrass, turn it up
I love you all, but

I am uncharitable. I
                        have
No love for you.

I am here, on this porch.
        The radio is plastic.
There is a plastic kazoo
There is
A shiny Lawson gutbucket.
The singer has a tiki round his neck
But he does not really come from California

There is music.
There was.
We have cut off our ears.
        My

Fucking father!
The door is open

Nobody is afraid of the razor strop
Hanging, the nail in the closet
The braid rug on the wall.
It makes me

I cannot
Make out the way and is it
                    Trembling or
                    Just fumbling I have to know
These feelings are an arbitrary pack
Trussed in a town I never lived in

                    My body
Hangs around me
Like a street gang round a yokel from upstate
                    Each move I make
Flips back, I wince

Then I get tired
Getting around—from check to check—
I am in a car without lights at night
                    In an open field
                    Seeking the road.

When she turned aside
From coffee and went down

Inside, to get the train
Inside the black street

When you turned aside
And sliced your wrists like celery sticks
            They turned you out
            Into a white room

I lost thirty pounds
The need of talking went, the idea of food
            I thinned out
            Around my navel and my mouth

They said I looked younger
I was the well-kept place in a suburb
            What grew that no one cared for
            Thinned out, trimmed back, pruned.

❖

Under the searchlight of the sun
Full volume

I've got the Black station

            All the keys they have given my life
            To open and close the doors which held me
            Open and close the rooms that clothed me
            Enter enter and enter the cells of bank accounts
            The manual of arms performed each night

To please him
To start up the cancer machine
To walk the straight hall of impotence, keys
Of warm beds sprinkled with old china broken
Warm beds sprinkled with oiled steel, the M-1, in bits
This is my weapon, this is my gun
This is my weapon, this is my gun
Lockers loaded with jockstraps and Egyptian unguents
· Immense combinations which opened stars

I look in the mirror and get the "exact change"
I look in the mirror, which doubles distances
I have grown
Smaller and smaller, my mouth is a hole
My lips were taken long ago
For eyes they have fitted in balls of Syrian glass
That peer through slits in pillows the phlegm makes
Plumbing up from the swollen bags of sinuses
My nose is a cherry, it has dipped in many mugs
And there are stretch marks on my belly

Like vapor trails in a sunless sky
Out from the dead mouth of my navel.

This is the way I love myself
This is the naked body in the mirror.
Father! I am burned again
My ambition will not

Consume me. No
All it is
Is you go out and get hooked once more

The wafer dry-sealed on the roof of the mouth.

Rare bird the size of a pea
Up on the tower in Austin
To those of you
Below strolling into

These human arms.

SOME FLOWERS

Lilacs flower by old roads
and purple loosestrife in marshes by the sea
cool beads of sweat
bloom on the glass that brims with vin rosé
and carries in its bowl
one little flower of the sun

while shots from rooftops crack out mocking
and flames bloom
out from tenements, long tiger
lilies, Shiva's arms
slow cobras in the swirl of fire
we carry one another
house to house

and room to room
nerves unmotored by forbidden flowers

this friend too burned to hold a water glass
and when we lift him from the couch
we feel the heft of knowledge we may not hold onto
something that is earthly, heavy
in our bodies alone

or later mornings
when the moist street gives back
a golden litter from the sun
we plunge ahead, as the light
changes, against ourselves.

NOTHING, NOTHING AT ALL

To be the diamond on the hilt of a sword
I have at length misplaced beyond recall;
To feel no more, because I am loved enough
And I return as much: like letters of credit

This joy entitles me; like a license to vend
Dark wines. To his beloved, man is a rainbow
Visible only from the other side
Of the weather of which he is the sign,

Of the sun of which he is reflection.
You see you are the poem you disregard,
You see that what you have not given up
At last not even memory could hold.

All that remains to be relinquished now
Is what you always held out for, this desire
To be desired, which keeps and tops the rim
Of any wellhead you had ever prized.

BRIDGE OF ABANDONMENT

to Anne Sexton

The door was painted on the wall

In your room you worked
The filing cabinet
Mining the load
Of memorabilia

Your Death, dressed like the good Gray Poet
Still leaned over your shoulder
Biting your neck
Leaving a brown-out hickey, token
Of ashen skylines
The seven bridges of a sexy life
Black moon blazoning a white shield

Still somewhere up the heart
There'd be another year for crooning
In spite of zeroes of monoxide

Clear water in cold light
Treading old rocks that make
Strong water hardly ripple
Brim or curl

Made a thing to wonder at

Black door, white wall.

THE LAST OF THE WALLENDAS

Another night, the dapper
Anthology of stars lights up.
The constellations, those jam pots
The young in their political beards
Raise gymnast pyramids toward.

✧

By Saturday at two the ancient allegiances
The stroked and the unstroked
Called out to remind us

Of a bronze-age glade
Where even the stuffed toys
Were fitted out by Puvis de Chavannes.

✧

Holding your arms in mine
One weight describing
The brother arc
From balance to balance,
Or back to back
To breathe, filling each other through
Solder of sweat
With arms outstretched we took
The lash of applause from the dark
Pit below. You spoke

Joy to have no guard to have
The courage to enact it

Not just talk about it.
It is I who have been unlike you
Dreaming hard
When searchlights singled us
Wired for thrills
As if we were an enemy
Within their wall.
Our act is finished.
Who was I
To you but your loss
Your twin
The ground you gave?

❖

Listen; the stone in the mill is grunting,
The voice from the river calls still.
In your own smile smiled over
Your own bounds
Was the suture that held.

❖

High between
Two buildings

The old man, blue
As a Chagall angel,
Is falling
The outline of
His body so small

Like an ankh
And the open mouth
Grinning or
Crying out,
"How I wanted you
Boys to know
I believed
The lines of my life."

SUMMER MOUNTAINS

1

ONCE AT MY WORK I KNEW A MASTER WATCHING

Noon sun reflected from the science
Building is seeping in my room
Across the desk, the light
Worn once already is going bare.
And there, a note:

> *Dear Stephen*
> *I am without a mind today*
> *I have been without*
> *A mind for a long time*
> *But today would be*
> *Agony   —Larry.*

Misery? —Silence
Waits at the office door.
At the planed cherry panel
Light gathers
When I move

Distant nebulae within
Gleam and reach out. When I move once more
In the grain's crest a wing flares
And an eye,
The wing swoops

A shower of cells accepting sunlight
And turns
Into the deep

And matter of dark fiber.
But now if I turn again

Out of the tree it shines forth,
The light passes near, to be touched
As if my being there
Like a climate watching from a throne of silence
Called the light wing forth

And comes to me
To my body, to urge the gleam's escape
From the manhandled polished plane
From sunless depth
Strident, yearning, airless within.

2

Across the Smoke-Stained Night I Saw

Blue stones rose
In the spaced flares as
If timed,
Burst from the barn, rhythmical

      midnight down
Imploding. From our hilltop
That November end the glow
Overhead joined

With a nimbus on cloud of village
          lights downvalley,

          you were drawn
To go down. Sprays of flame & boughs
Of sparks showered against
East Mountain, inkswirls of night
          where the circle of faces watching
Watched what they all had long awaited:
          a building passing
As if in anger, in wonder, one
          derelict twisting upon itself
Toward zero. A coal losing tensile
Stresses opening
Igneous sun cleavings

Meant
Not finality, scarlet reduction
For women in coats   men in jackshirts
On watch to see between
          hope and hope if
It would spread. This ward
Was theirs
If it belonged to none they knew

The crown   the plentiful menace.

✧

You make me see this
November end of years ago
            in from setting out seedlings
            chives   parsley   basil

Watching the photograph Sarah gave you
The stream along Route 9
Where 1/10th of one second caught
            the flow the
Wavelet surge and downrush
Mountain snow water turning
The spill to feathery
            flames
            in this print
Over a shallow bed of stones lucent
                  diffracted a little and
                  so
                  appearing to join
                  in the onward pull
Of the pelf, the presence, liquid
Of turning out, the local
Haste of caught
Water   caught as flame
Over earth's gleaming
            rounded stones:

This in the camera's reversing take
And the plate of acids
Getting the colors of it in
            leaving them out

The stream's time
A glimpse of inside-fear
                    animal
Fur streaking to cover
                    among arching leaves.

Can you see it now?
As cloud like a slick
Calming the measureless elements in a wide
Circle through vortical sky,

Space that needs time?

                    ❖

Or, let us agree
While our vales and senses meet

A stream taken
Out of time by
This picture, this *take*

"To be
Perceived"
And that time taken
In   as a streaming
Over solid stones

                    is
                    as our proper love
                    when the bright maneuver

                              of interceding song one moment
                                   quenches desire
                                   and desire.

And yet
          orages:
In their steelyard eyes those strangers held
Microversions of the flames.
Flaring in each wide eye
The townsfolk took that burning
That breaking up
                    that burning inward
Their fire, luck, victory.

                         The bright maneuver
                         of its taking leave
                         and final singing

                         beams that were
                         limbs collapsing in
                         as the sparks fly up!

That this should have come to me
On June the 3rd!

Gripping us all once
in staccato holes
unforeseen divisions

to mean / is
to be forgot

and the blue stones
rose.

3

I Picked a Flower One Evening in America

On ground below
        the clouds streaming away
That dark
        clarifying

One great
        lotus at zenith
I picked a flower
        fumbled for stem

I could not find
        brown by day

September grasses
    with weed stalks

Steadying the steady
    monochrome
Of night
    eyes caromed on

Searching for seamark there
    red or any color
Eyeless I chose
    that flower

Mercifully chose me
    lay in my palm
O differently last night
    from earth it grew

Open and night
    and not to be believed
It counseled me
    of silence

One evening in America
    of openings
Downward under
    thighs

Of the dark earth
    chasms in my head

Holding wide
	a mirror image

Distances doubled
	by thought
When there above
	my head where

No cloud longer was
	linear corridors of war
Bubble across the night
	scarring a moon

A sum
	a serpent trailing
Scum
	long over cosmic oceans

The contrails string
	above my head
With grass for pillow
	moonlight limestone

Beside my head
	at crotches of a daisy stem
His spittled egg
	the moss snail smears

The ancient
	sexual rage of generals

In after-burn
        streak of glow

Worm O simple
        moon riding
Styro-
        foam sheetings now

And now the rose
        mouth sick
Of Moloch
        gagging

On the white
        alum of unmanned knowledge.
The edge of light
        scores dark's horizon

Rising and wind
        returned without assurance
Weeping
        this hill so wet

A red flower
        lies shattered in the grass
A little flail
        of flame out

Out as the wine moon
    takes back its beams
Vanishes with clouds
    toward dawn

While the whole earth
    each brush of straw
The tiny galaxies of
    calico aster

Lean toward their dark
    the deep grain
Of their season
    magmas of mist swirl

Vine quill
    wet wind downvalley
Leaf curl weed tumble
    sea spray of frost.

4

SPUN WITH THE INTENSITY OF WILLFUL SLEEP

He could drive no longer
And he pulled to the shoulder
Lay out on the grass

Supine under wind, longing
And saw armadas of the clouds advance
Crossing a sea of space above.

When all was one
Instant stilled
    and was
His body on the breast of earth
    and the earth
The whole globe of men and stones
That heaved in unrelenting turns
And deep space in grid of cloud
    stood off

He sensed in that wide deep
A force as if a presence
    with an eye
That looked down showers of pure light
From veridical zenith
      inerrant being
Pouring a stillness of repose that mocked
His liquid eye's mistake
    and all his body
Pulled by comfort to grass
    a green, jackstraw
Ixion to a planet staked
    stuffed with untender sticks
And ready tinder, with need

To find himself an axis
        of a blasted planet
Hardly sounding as it slowly turned.

Sun warmed the confusing body then
And then supine already
He lay there with arms outstretched
More easily lay all him down
And turned with the planet as it turned
Under the canopy of cloud unmoving
Of clouds hung motionless above
And turned with the planet as it turned

Remembered
And remembered the one moment
When neither cloud nor he had moved
And found that what he thought he saw
        or saw he thought
Meant only he might see
        what he might cast before him
As a tree
May not move from its one place
Save in the generations that go out from it
        when seasons pass
In haste among its limbs:

        he stood
Drove away up the sheering highway

Did not stop for one who stood there
  gesturing to be taken up
Motionless on the shoulder when he sped by

Until he saw him in the mirror there
A twin of darkness diminishing to horizon
And he turned around and back again
  into his old path
Becoming this fellow
  traveler's ride.

THE PAINTER

Obsession with surfaces still held an odor
Of life, even if a shameful or despairing life.
How could he be anything else than his
Encounter with the world? "The flayed ox" appears

And reappears, like the mirage it is. The meaning
Of that yellow rent in the sky remains the captive
Of its color, sure. It was as if each argument
Was a facade without interiors, like a stage

With niches, doorways leading nowhere, engaged columns
Engaged without a purpose, all for show.
The painting, like a regatta, suggests a progress
Of ideas, but it is only play, however earnest.

"Goodness knows what he was looking at,"
The innkeeper would say in confidential tones
To patrons who might improve his story. "The nude
Women were bathing in some other place."

RETURNING TO EAGLE BRIDGE

It is time for the inaccessible again,
To lose the place, and all that had taken place.
On the terrace the myrtle is creeping on the marble
Slab we unearthed by the barn and planted here
Face-up so its buried words would see the light,
"H. Pratt" and "Fecit, 1 8 7 8."
The grooves uneven, graved by an amateur,
Seem fainter now after seven years of rain,
Just legible—before the myrtle had begun
Its evergreen erasure. Names everywhere
Here; everywhere lost track of, as if
Some Berlin Wall turning everyone back invaded
An indivisibility of years,
Of lives, lining us all with its red ink.

Your shadow falls like a winged seed that softly
Alights on the gravel. We see the old life here
Like a reverse view through a telescope, emotions
In miniature, gestures in a doll's house; each room
Stands as it did, but empty, the spaces loitering;
Sunlight on wide pine floors. A lid of stone
Lifting some turf, brow that we soon remember
Of the mountain below, is the tip of granite quilted
By grass where days absorbed us, patches of color
At play between the deep rock and a deep sky.
The cat—not the same cat, but on the same wall—
With his eyes open dreams the absence he'll be
One day when his nerves betray him, and he won't find
His way to this door. The wind pulls at the vine
By the chimney; soon you answer, "it is time to go in."

Next month new tenants will peer from windows and
  wonder
Who found this land and knew it to be good,
Cleared these billowing hills, hewed each joist,
Raised walls and hollowed out the cistern rock;
Generation and generation dreaming
Under the low eaves, wading in Fern Brook,
Fishing from Low Bridge Road; finding one day
In the glass their tall bodies settling downward
From the shoulders, the pull of earth, the downward arc.
The child who knew our great oak as a sapling
Is gone, the girl he picnicked with on Cedar Hill
Lies by him still, *Patient till God. Ruth Safford*
Pratt. 1810–1890.
In the rooms once more unfurnished they'll watch where
  pines
Fill up the pasture; sumac and goldenrod,
Poplar and cherry sealing the dry-stone walls.

A storm front, as this cloud pulsing now, may seethe
From behind the ridge into view above, turning
The grass pale, tossing the bare maples, sending
Our swallows to soar and dive on the veering hawk.
The storm prow heads off; at the window now a whirlpool
Of leaves flying anywhere. We knew contentment
In this place, but Eagle Bridge had other plans;
A crowded mountainside, though vacant, where
Moonlight blazes the tree limbs. We try as we can
And think of christening the child born in the room
Behind our kitchen, our child who sleeps outside

The circle, but the thought keeps slipping off
Like the red fox that gnawed our garbage and, filled,
Lurked off uphill by moonlight to his vixen.

In this parlor fathers whiled their winters into March
Padding the Belgian carpet in carpet slippers,
Believing and believing behind the heavy drapes,
Watching the black, crisp curls of flies startle
In the window sash as the storm raged. The shadows
Of branches tangle on the wall behind us; in the moonlight
The wall we stripped the blue-rose paper from
And painted white shines, white as an appliance;
The plaster seems to unfurl in the restless shadows,
To grow, fuzzing as moss grows, out from the wall.
We ask who first abandoned the rusty stanchions
Or look for the outlines of cows drowsing the field
Where once we thought we saw a child who shouldered
A mullein stalk and marched for hours between
Milkhouse and barn. Tonight the shades of all
The people who have dined in this room tiptoe
Backward into the unsilvering dust-scarved mirrors
Or, backing against the wallpaper (blue roses
On red, foxed with the browns of sudden downpours)
Stand motionless until they vanish into
The dusky scarlets and tear-stained blues, step backward
Into the shadows or out the doors, willing
And unwilling (as with any country forsaking)
But going, as a bee through clover, regardlessly
Without a thought of what has used him so well.
In his sleep our son cries out as his teeth probe,